The Guide to the Circular Economy

Capturing Value and Managing Material Risk

Dustin Benton

Head of Energy and Resources, Green Alliance

dbenton@green-alliance.org.uk

Jonny Hazell

Senior Policy Adviser, Green Alliance

jhazell@green-alliance.org.uk

Julie Hill

Associate, Green Alliance

jhill@green-alliance.org.uk

Routledge
Taylor & Francis Group

LONDON AND NEW YORK

First published 2014 by Greenleaf Publishing Limited

Published 2017 by Routledge
2 Park Square, Milton Park, Abingdon, Oxon OX14 4RN
711 Third Avenue, New York, NY 10017, USA

*Routledge is an imprint of the Taylor & Francis Group,
an informa business*

ISBN 978-1-910174-35-7 (pbk)

A catalogue record for this title is available from the British Library.

Page design and typesetting by Alison Rayner
Cover by Becky Chilcott

Abstract

THE TERM 'CIRCULAR ECONOMY' is becoming familiar to an increasing number of businesses. It expresses an aspiration to get more value from resources and waste less, especially as resources come under a variety of pressures – price-driven, political and environmental. Delivering the circular economy brings direct costs savings, reduces risk, brings reputational advantages and can therefore be a market differentiator. But working out what counts as 'circular' activity for an individual business, as against the entire economy or individual products, is not straightforward. This book demystifies the language of the circular economy, and gives examples to show what it looks like in practice. It also equips readers to make the links between their own company's initiatives and those of others, making those activities count by influencing actors across the supply chain.

About the Authors

DUSTIN BENTON started with Green Alliance in June 2011, and runs the Low Carbon Energy and Resource Stewardship themes. His role includes responsibility for work on energy efficiency and renewables, the UK's electricity market, and carbon capture and storage (CCS), alongside work on resource scarcity and the Circular Economy Task Force. Before joining Green Alliance, Dustin worked for the Campaign to Protect Rural England where he led work on the relationship between landscape protection, climate change and new energy infrastructure. He also led on the future of land use, and was a key contributor to CPRE's Vision for the Countryside, which provides a long-term perspective on how the countryside should be managed in the light of increasing demands on the land. He holds an MA in political thought and theory from the University of Birmingham and an MA in international relations and French from the University of St Andrews.

JONNY HAZELL joined Green Alliance in June 2012 to support the Resource Stewardship theme. He works with Dustin Benton and associate Julie Hill on the Circular Economy Task Force. Before joining Green Alliance he was research director at Inovenergy where he worked on 'The 1 Tonne Roadshow', an event series exploring and promoting best practice in waste management. He also led research projects on the UK's renewable heat market, and consultancy work on promoting the reuse of materials in London and social enterprise in China. He holds an MSc in nature, society and environmental policy and a BA in experimental psychology, both from the University of Oxford.

 **JULIE HILL** is a former Director and now Associate of Green Alliance. In November 2014 she was appointed Chair of WRAP UK, and had previously chaired the Circular Economy Task Force, a group of eight leading businesses, including WRAP. She is also a member of the board of the Consumer Council for Water and a fellow of the University of Surrey. She has previously been a member of the board of the Eden Project in Cornwall and the Environment Agency for England and Wales. She is the author of *The Secret Life of Stuff* published by Vintage Books in 2011.

Acknowledgments

THIS BOOK would not have been possible without the support of the Circular Economy Task Force, a group of eight leading businesses convened by Green Alliance. The first phase of the Task Force, running from July 2012 to July 2014, held discussions that informed many of the topics in this book – resource risks and the need for resilience, the motivations for moving towards a more circular economy, barriers to change, key metrics, and finding the right scale for the circular economy. The Task Force first and second year reports are available at: **http:// www.green-alliance.org.uk/CETF.php**.

Thanks are also due to those who reviewed drafts: Alison Austin, Patrick Mahon, Nick Morley, Jenny Stafford, James Walker, Markus Zils and everyone who helped with case studies.

....

Contents

Preface

THIS BOOK IS FOR:

- Business leaders.

- Sustainability professionals wanting to progress specific circular economy goals within their organisations.

- Brand managers and public affairs practitioners wanting an introduction to the concept.

- Professionals at all levels seeking recipes for action.

- Financial institutions looking for future investment opportunities.

- Anyone who wants to understand what difference we can make to global resource use.

What you should get out of reading this book:

- Feel stimulated by the businesses opportunities presented by a new economic model.

- See the circular economy in a political and business context; understand where it has come from and where it is going.

- A sophisticated understanding of material risk and the means to embed that into corporate practice.

- Understand the debate around metrics and indicators to assess your current level of circularity, set priorities and measure success.

- Understand what conditions have enabled other companies to change the system in which they operate.

....

Introduction –
A New Model for
Business and Society

A CIRCULAR ECONOMY is one where the resources coming into the economy are not allowed to become waste or lose their value. Instead, this economy would recover those resources and keep them in productive use for as long as possible.

The opposite of a circular economy is a linear economy: extract raw materials, produce goods, sell them, use them and throw them away. To a large extent, this is where we are now, particularly in the Western, developed economies. This model has been made possible by abundant natural resources, cheap labour and cheap or free means of disposal. But as all parts of the world catch up with Western levels of consumption, and populations grow, none of these conditions can be taken for granted.

Below are some statistics used to demonstrate the scale of the losses from the economy in the form of wasted resources. Each of them also represents a business opportunity.

- The UK puts £3.8 billion worth of resources into landfill every year (Green Alliance: **www.green-alliance.org.uk/landfillbans. php**). **Opportunity?** With investment in the right infrastructure for recovery, new markets will evolve for these products and materials.

- The UK's food and drink supply chain produces 15 million tonnes of food waste per year (WRAP: **www.wrap.org.uk/food-waste-reduction**) and, globally, nearly a third of all the food produced is wasted somewhere the supply chain (FAO: **www.unep.org/wed/2013/quickfacts/**). **Opportunities?** In technologies and techniques for smarter food production, better food preservation and better logistics. Also clever chemistry to turn organic waste into chemicals, fertilisers and fuels.

- US women own $550 worth of clothes they have never worn (VoucherCloud: **www.huffingtonpost.com/2014/03/28/unworn-clothing-survey_n_5048486.html**). **Opportunity?** The development of alternative businesses models such as the leasing of clothes.

- There is a floating mass of plastic waste in the Pacific Ocean measuring somewhere between 0.7 and 15 million square kilometres, the latter being 8 percent of the area of the ocean (Wikipedia: **http://en.wikipedia.org/wiki/Great_Pacific_garbage_patch**). **Opportunity?** For developing means of recovering and using this material, along with many other instances of materials currently thought to be beyond recovery.

- Around a third of all washing machines and fridges, and a quarter of all the vacuum cleaners replaced in the UK each year failed to meet the average customer's expectation for each product's lifetime (WRAP: **www.wrap.org.uk/content/switched-value**). **Opportunity?** Selling products with longer lifetimes, easier repair, leasing arrangements and extended warranties.

This book aims to excite the reader by laying out these opportunities, and by providing practical steps along the way to more circular business models.

....

Getting Hold of the Key Concepts

No. 1: **Our economies are underpinned by natural resources**

WE MAKE, BUY AND SELL STUFF, and the stuff has to come from somewhere. Everything we use is either grown or mined, and everything tracks back to the physical sources of these raw materials – be they food, timber, fibres, metals, minerals, or the oil that gives us fuel, plastics and chemicals.

TABLE 1. Some resources terminology

Resources	The basics that underpin all of our life and economies – **land, raw materials, energy, water.** Land and water tend to be the hardest to substitute.
Biotic resources	Sources of materials and energy that come from **plants or animals**, whether farmed or wild – food, wood, paper, textiles such as cotton, wool and leather. Also generally thought of as 'renewable' – i.e. they grow and can replace themselves or are replaced through farming and forestry. Although these resources are renewable, many are under as much pressure from increasing consumption as non-renewable resources.

Abiotic resources	The **mined resources** – metals and minerals. Oil and coal are interesting as they were once biological materials (animals and plants) but as they are now fossil resources and not renewable, they tend to get classified with the mined resources. This means that plastics from oil (they can also be made from plants) come into this camp.
Primary and secondary resources	Primary are the resources coming straight from agriculture, forestry and mining. Secondary resources have been reclaimed from their first use.
Natural capital	All the stuff the planet provides that we take – from fish to forests to grazing land to minerals. A term used to make the point that without these basic resources, we wouldn't be able to generate monetary capital.
Ecosystem services	The **'life support systems'** of the planet provided by natural areas – e.g. water and nutrient cycling, a stable climate, green space, natural beauty and recreation. These 'services' are also considered to be a part of 'natural capital'.
'Stuff'	Rather unspecific, but generally conjures up **materials and products** rather than energy and water, and is a friendly term used to make people think about their personal consumption of materials.
Resource criticality	The idea that some **specific resources are critical to a particular economy's success** and may be subject to supply restrictions. These are often 'niche' (specialised and/or small quantity) but high-value materials that are central to particular technologies – for instance, the indium in touch screens or 'rare earth' metals in magnets.

Bioeconomy	A new term expressing the aspiration to shift the source of economic value from non-renewable resources to **renewable resources.** Biofuels and biomass sources of energy are one strand of this debate, but more economic value may be gained from applications in materials and chemicals.

No. 2: **Resources are becoming less 'secure' for a variety of reasons**

FIGURE 1. Price increases of three basic commodities against inflation, 2003–2012

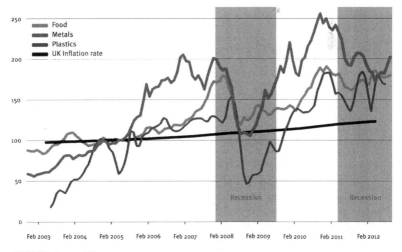

SOURCE: Green Alliance

These are the converging trends and concerns that have helped to increase interest in the circular economy:

- A reversal in the trend of the last four decades of declining **resource prices**. The prices of food, metals and plastics of have risen in the last eight years faster than background inflation, and continued rising through a recession.

- Not only are prices rising, they are more **volatile**, with bigger spikes and troughs. This uncertainty is a big problem for businesses, stifling investment and inhibiting confident forward planning.

- Underlying these price trends are **environmental pressures** – although the basic metals, for instance, will not 'run out' any time soon, the increasing energy and water needed to access more dilute sources drives up costs.

- One of the factors underlying food price rises and limiting a shift to using more bio-based or 'renewable' materials is the competition for high quality agricultural **land** (for food, fuels and materials).

- On top of this, there are fears of restrictions on **access** to key resources by political decisions – for instance, the Chinese Government restricting export of 'rare earth' minerals to keep them for their own use.

- As demand for resources rises, and prices become more volatile and strained, we may see more **resource nationalism** – an effort to stop flows of key resources outside a country under stress.

- At the same time, the world is facing **increasing demand** for resources as global population rises, and the affluence of that population increases.

- **Climate change** may mean a less predictable climate, disrupting access to raw materials and water. In response there are moves in several countries to regulate or price carbon emissions, which would have further impacts on energy and resource prices.

- These aren't just abstract risks – putting a proper price on **carbon** (i.e. around €75 per tonne) would cause the price of primary aluminium to rise by 70 percent, chromium to rise by 240 percent and nylon to rise by 40 percent.

FIGURE 2. Percentage price rise of materials if the cost of carbon is included

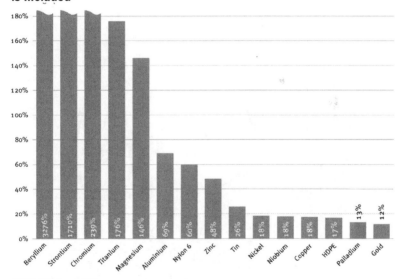

SOURCE: Green Alliance

- Companies are subject to increasing scrutiny of their supply chains by consumers and by campaigning groups, and their **reputations** are at risk in the event that environmental or social problems associated with their raw materials are uncovered. Recent high profile campaigns on conflict minerals, palm oil and coal-fired electricity in computer data-centres are prime examples. Social media means that there is nowhere to hide.

No. 3: Circular economy thinking gives companies more options in the face of resource insecurity

FIGURE 3. Keeping value in a circular economy

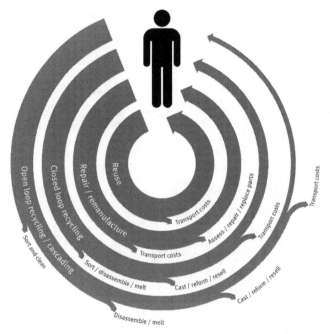

SOURCE: Green Alliance

A circular economy approach encourages companies to look at their operations and their supply chains, and think about how resources are sourced, how they can be used more efficiently, where they can be more effectively recovered, and where the need for raw materials can be designed out of the business model altogether. Together these strategies add up to greater understanding and control of the supply chain, reducing exposure to resource risks, avoiding reputational threats and eliminating waste.

Figure 3 shows that the nearer to their original state products and materials can be kept, by re-use and remanufacturing, the more value can be captured because of the avoidance of processing, transport and other costs.

Examples of these strategies include:

- **Leasing products** to consumers is being examined as a new business model by many companies, extending it away from the current high value examples, such as cars and large industrial equipment, towards more everyday items such as appliances and clothes. Leasing creates an incentive for companies to recover the products and materials and get repeated value from them, while offering consumers the service they want, and assuring them of minimal waste. There are examples below under Step 2.

- **Re-use** is perhaps the most obvious but most neglected strategy, one which can involve complexity to establish, but then substantial financial savings. For instance, Sainsbury's has a comprehensive re-use centre for equipment from its stores, established with the help of its facilities management company. This is now a highly successful and cost-effective operation (see Box on page 30 for more detail).

- **Remanufacturing**, which involves restoring a product to a like-new or better status, is a good strategy for companies where they are producing complex, higher value products. Siemens, GE and Philips all remanufacture medical imaging equipment such as scanners, and digger company Caterpillar (**www.caterpillar.com/ en/company/brands/cat-reman.html**) has a much-quoted and highly profitable remanufacturing model. Remanufacturing is one of the least visible of the 'circular strategies', as its products are indistinguishable from new.

- Helping companies to establish **'closed loops'** opens up new business opportunities. An increasing trend for joint venture arrangements has boosted business for plastics recyclers, for instance. Closed Loop Recycling (**www.closedlooprecycling.co.uk/ blog/ms-and-the-circular-economy.php**), a company established to recycle PET bottles back into PET bottles, is based on a partnership between companies with demand for a recycled product (for instance, M&S), and a provider with the sorting technology to supply PET (Veolia). Similarly, the rapidly growing UK recycler ECO plastics (www.ecoplasticsltd.com/default.aspx) quadrupled its capacity between 2009 and 2014. With the help of Viridor and other joint ventures, it is supplying Coca Cola (**www. coca-cola.co.uk/environment/coca-cola-eco-plastics-recycling-joint-venture.html**).

- **Internal recycling** is often overlooked and can yield significant energy and financial benefits. In Japan, flat panel display manufacturers collect indium (**www.japanfs.org/en/news/ archives/news_id026099.html**) tin oxide wasted in the production process and send it for recycling in a closed loop process that ensures that the reprocessor sends it back to the original manufacturers.

- Even obvious recycling strategies such as recovering steel can be improved with thoughtful use of **information**. Shipping line Maersk (www.worldslargestship.com/facts/cradle-to-cradle/) publishes a 'product passport' for its new ships showing where different grades of metals are used – the separation of these alloys that this makes possible has raised the value of their recycling by 10 percent.

- Replacing key raw materials with **recovered alternatives** can mean greater certainty of price or supply, as well as have reputational benefits. This will be increasingly true for plastics, where a combination of exposure to the price of oil, increased global consumption and consumer pressure to prevent plastic waste reaching the environment, offers big growth opportunities for those such as international company MBA Polymers (**www. mbapolymers.com/home/**) investing in plastic recovery.

- Where carbon is priced, this will eventually work through to the **'embedded' carbon** in products, making them more expensive. **Recycled aluminium** would rise by just 7 percent compared to 70 percent for primary material, and companies re-using or buying remanufactured goods made of this material would be almost entirely protected from price rises. Even where carbon is not priced, rising energy costs in many parts of the world make these strategies beneficial.

The Sainsbury's re-use centre

The re-use centre came out of Sainsbury's Zero Waste to Landfill objective, and realising that store equipment had no easy route for re-use. In partnership with Sainsbury's facilities management company, Fit Out (UK), the initiative identified storage space and set up a reverse logistics system whereby lorries delivering new kit to stores bring equipment back to the reuse centre. From there, a large range of appliances and fittings including ovens, fridges, shelving and displays can be cleaned, returned to manufacturers for repair or refurbishment if necessary, and upgraded wherever possible. The equipment is then logged on the web-based re-use system and advertised to other stores, with managers required to look for a re-used item before ordering new. The system has saved more than £1 million. Key to success has been leadership from high up in the organisation, effective reverse logistics, and providing users with confidence, through standards, that equipment will perform as new.

What is the difference between reuse, remanufacturing and recycling?

The Centre for Reuse and Remanufacturing (**www.oakdenehollins. co.uk/newsdetail.php?which=134**) has some helpful definitions.

Reuse encompasses a range of activities where whole products (or whole parts of products) are used again in one piece. This includes:

- Straight reuse (probably by someone else!), possibly in a different way.

- Refurbishment – cleaning, lubricating or other improvement.

- Repair – rectifying a fault.

- Redeployment and cannibalisation – using working parts elsewhere.

Remanufacturing is 'a series of manufacturing steps acting on an end-of-life part or product in order to return it to like-new or better performance, with warranty to match'.

Remanufacturing is the only option that requires a full treatment process – like new manufacture – to guarantee the performance of the finished object. As such it necessarily involves more effort, time and cost – but you do get the quality guarantee.

Remanufacturing is different from recycling because, as with all product reuse options, it involves preserving (or indeed improving) the whole product and its function. In contrast, recycling activities require the destruction of the product to its component materials so they can be melted, smelted or reprocessed into new forms.

Examples of remanufactured products include engines, machine tools, photocopiers, computers, defence equipment, carpet tiles and trains. Remanufacturing is a good option for complex, durable products of higher value.

See also this Parliamentary report about the benefits of remanu-facturing from the APSRG (**www.policyconnect.org.uk/apsrg/ sites/site_apsrg/files/apsrg_-_remanufacturing_report.pdf**).

No. 4: **The economy-wide benefits are also likely to be considerable**

- Recovery of more resources, keeping them in stock or in 'loops' rather than losing them as 'waste', should reduce the need for primary extraction (which is still likely to grow, but as not as much as it might do under 'business as usual). It should also reduce, or at least delay, the need to dispose of 'waste'.

- Recovering products that have come from overseas and contain 'critical' and price volatile materials, and keeping them in use in the UK, could help UK industry hedge against future volatility or political restrictions on these materials. This could be particularly important if politicians want to encourage significant 're-shoring' of manufacturing in the UK or elsewhere in Europe, ensuring the UK retains and maximises its competitive advantage.

- We now have the data to show how much embedded energy (and therefore carbon emissions) and water are involved in making and selling products. Any waste prevention of a product or its materials through reuse and recycling is a saving of this energy, carbon and water, which is a global economic benefit, even though those benefits might not accrue directly to the company making or distributing the product, or the country where it is based.

No. 5: **The circular economy can be local, national, or global**

One of the problems with the concept of the circular economy is visualising where it is. Walter Stahel of the Geneva-based Product Life Institute, to many people the 'father' of circular economy, sees regional scale (sub-units of countries) as the most appropriate and manageable. This is where co-operation between companies might be easiest to organise and control, and yield the most benefits – but that doesn't mean that more local and even global circles can't also work well.

Figuring out what is the best scale for a circular economy ultimately rests on the balance between the value of a product or material, and the cost of transport – as in any supply chain. Existing circular recycling systems for the precious metals in automotive catalysts for instance, are global, because precious metals are hugely valuable. Circular systems for remanufactured industrial engines and pumps are also global. In contrast, circular models for getting the most value out of food waste probably need to be very local to minimise the cost and environmental impact of moving heavy, low value organic material.

No. 6: **The circular economy idea has been reaching maturity over the last three decades**

The circular economy idea is not new. It was first sketched out by Walter Stahel (**www.product-life.org/en/about**), a Swiss architect, who in the 1970s came up with the idea of an economy in 'loops' that would recycle resources into productive use rather than losing them, and generate more jobs in the process. The idea is also central to the academic discipline of 'industrial ecology' which extends to the whole economy, the idea of industries using each other's waste products (termed 'industrial symbiosis') and studies the practical ways in which this can be made a reality. Also influential has been the 'Cradle to Cradle' (**www.c2ccertified.org/**) concept, promoted by German chemist Michael Braungart and American architect

Bill McDonough, where the aspiration is that everything is designed to be reclaimed and remade. The Japanese have also been central to the development of the circular economy, using 'producer responsibility' legislation: the makers of products are obliged to ensure that they are recovered and recycled. The Chinese are increasingly active, enacting a 'Circular Economy Law' in 2008 and with a rapidly growing academic literature on what it might mean for the Chinese economy (**https://www. zotero.org/groups/jie_citations/items/itemKey/JNQN7ZQ3**).

For the UK, important influences on circular economy thinking include European Directives aimed at the reduction and recycling of waste, as well as the work of the Waste and Resources Action Programme (WRAP) (**www. wrap.org.uk/**) to help develop markets for the materials collected from our households by local authorities, and materials collected from businesses. In Europe, we have gradually moved to a mentality focused on recovering value from discarded resources, and reducing environmental impacts at the same time, rather than a mentality concerned with regulating the negative impacts of waste. Progressing to a circular economy means moving further to a model which preserves as much as possible of the value of materials and products that we already have in the economy.

The concept of the circular economy has been hugely popularised by Dame Ellen MacArthur, the round-the-world yachtswoman, whose voyages underlined to her the importance of careful stewardship of scarce resources. She established a foundation to promote the business take-up of the circular economy, and ensure that the principles are embedded in our education system. The Ellen MacArthur Foundation (www.ellenmacarthurfoundation. org/) has commissioned ground-breaking research from economic analysts McKinsey and Co., which demonstrates the huge potential financial benefits of keeping resources in use. A complementary initiative is The Great Recovery Project (**www.greatrecovery.org.uk/**) run by the RSA in London, which has demonstrated the financial and reputational benefits of better design. The Green Alliance (**www.green-alliance.org.uk/**), a UK-based NGO, has formed coalitions with leading businesses (including the Circular Economy Task Force – **www.green-alliance.org.uk/CETF.php**) to ask Government for policy support for the circular economy. These messages have struck a chord at a time of increased concern about prices, volatility and future access to key resources.

Chapter recap: The 'elevator pitch' for the circular economy

- All economic activity depends on **resources**, whether obtained in one country or many, in short or long supply chains.

- These resources are increasingly **'insecure'** – not because they will physically run out, but because price, or other restrictions, will make access more difficult.

- Circular thinking offers ways to make better use of resources, and keep them in the **control** of your business.

- It also offers wider **economic and environmental** benefits.

- Circular systems may be **local, regional or global**.

- This is **not a new idea** – it has been developed and refined over decades.

STEP 2

Seeing the Benefits and Interpreting Them to Colleagues: Some Case Studies

THESE ARE SOME EXAMPLES to illustrate leading businesses' reasons for considering circular economy approaches.

1. Economic resilience

The global company Unilever (**www.unilever.com/sustainable-living-2014/reducing-environmental-impact/waste-and-packaging/Reduce-Reuse-Recycle/**) has undertaken thorough supply chain analysis in pursuit of greater resource efficiency. Its 2014 update reported cumulative supply chain savings of over €350 million. Of these savings, €182 million was for material savings, more than the energy saved (€153 million) and more than ten times the avoided cost of waste disposal (€17 million). Examples include using more recycled plastic in its products, reducing the amount of aluminium in an aerosol can by 25 percent through improved design, and using new technology to inject gas bubbles into plastic packaging, enabling the material to be reduced by 15 percent, while leaving the package fully recyclable.

Communications services company BT (**www.bt.com/betterfuture**) has seen the cost-saving benefits of analysing the footprints of some its key products, and of engaging with its supply chain by setting procurement standards for all suppliers. These and other measures have, as reported in a Carbon Trust (**www.carbontrust.com/media/468325/ ctc828-opportunities-in-a-resource-constrained-world.pdf**) report, yielded a:

44% reduction in operational carbon emissions and a 15% reduction in supply chain emissions, along with a 40% reduction in waste to landfill since 2011. At the same time, BT has decreased operating costs by 14% and boosted EBITDA by 6% – building a strong investment in the company's future and that of the UK's telecommunications infrastructure.

The Ellen MacArthur Foundation asked the global consulting firm McKinsey and Company (**www.ellenmacarthurfoundation.org/business/ reports**) to analyse the financial benefits of different circular economy strategies for a selection of products. One of the top benefits was for mobile phones. McKinsey looked at the benefits of increasing collection rates of used phones from 15 to 50 percent, and designing phones to be more easily disassembled to re-use the components if the whole phone can't be re-used. If 50 percent of devices were collected (and of those, 38% are reused, 41% are remanufactured and 21% are recycled), market-wide savings on manufacturing material costs could add up to $1 billion (about 30% of total industry material input costs), and manufacturing energy costs savings to $60 million (about 16% of total industry energy input costs) a year. In an advanced scenario with 95 percent collection and an equal split between reuse and remanufacturing, material and energy savings could be as much as $2 billion on material and $160 million on energy annually.

2. New business opportunities

Changing the business model from ownership to access

Car clubs for short-trip car rental are becoming a familiar model, with companies such as Zipcar and Easycar growing strongly over the last decade. Zipcar UK (**www.zipcar.co.uk/node/37336?gclid=CJ-YlKqcns ICFQvJtAodtwcALQ**) estimates that every rental car on the street replaces six privately owned cars, making better use of those resources, and saves members an average of £300 per month compared to car owners.

McKinsey Consulting (**www.ellenmacarthurfoundation.org/business/ toolkit/in-depth-washing-machines**) has projected that high-end washing machines would be accessible for most households if they were leased instead of sold – customers would save roughly a third per wash cycle, and the manufacturer would earn roughly a third more in profits. Over a 20-year period, replacing the purchase of five 2000-cycle machines with leases of one 10,000-cycle machine would also yield almost 180 kg of steel savings and more than 2.5 tonnes of CO_2e savings.

Dutch firm Mud Jeans (**http://nl.mudjeans.eu/**) leases jeans and hooded tops, both manufactured in Italy, on a yearly basis. Customers return the jeans, choose new ones, or pay a bit extra to keep them at the end of the year. It also runs a vintage line to sell second-hand jeans returned by leasers at the end of the contract. There is a small economic saving to the consumer, but the main attraction is ensuring that the clothes are kept in circulation as long as possible (textiles are one of the hardest waste streams to recycle effectively, and re-use is a much better option). Also the company can market itself as 'fair fashion'.

At the other end of the fashion market, New York-based company Rent the Runway (**https://www.renttherunway.com/story**) has created a rapidly growing online means of leasing designer clothes. It employs a reverse logistics model to dispatch and collect garments, making the leasing process easy and enjoyable for customers. The company declares that 'access is the new ownership' and the *New York Times* has described it as 'a Netflix model for haut couture'.

Leading outdoor clothing manufacturer Patagonia (**www.patagonia. com/us/common-threads/**) has made a virtue of clothes that last a long time, pledges to help customers repair them, offers space in its stores and online to sell used items, and takes back clothes for recycling if they are beyond repair.

Kyocera: Setting a new design and service standard for user benefit

Printer company **KYOCERA's Ecosys** printers are designed to be highly resource efficient. Most companies' printer cartridges contain the print drum, developer unit and fuser as well as the toner powder – up to 60 different parts made of a range of materials – which are all replaced every time the toner runs out. Kyocera has designed its system so that the print drum, developer and fuser are permanent parts of the printer, designed for greater durability and guaranteed to last their entire design life. As a result, only the toner powder has to be replaced regularly. This results in the printer being in effect 'cartridge-free'. For the customer, the benefits are lower consumables costs and longer maintenance intervals, as well as knowing that the equipment has a better environmental footprint than its rivals. The advanced design means a 55 percent reduction in carbon footprint, 85 percent reduction in waste and a consumables cost saving of typically 54 percent.

This system also avoids the raw materials, manufacturing and transport impacts of the components that are no longer part of a consumable. (When a conventional print cartridge is 'remanufactured', these parts would have to be replaced as they aren't designed for extended use and would otherwise fail or compromise print quality.)

The Ecosys printers are also designed for easy disassembly (more on disassembly below). Metal fixings are minimised and all screws have the same head. Plastic parts simply clip together and are embossed to show where to apply pressure to detach them. The company is looking at how it can ensure that used printers are channelled to companies who can do this disassembly, so as to get the full value from the parts, rather than just shred the equipment for recycling, as happens to most e-waste collected through WEEE compliance schemes. This pioneering work with the supply chain will ultimately result in an even better circular system for the printers.

KYOCERA has capitalised further on this resource-efficient design by using it as the basis for managed document services. These allow companies to have printing and copying capability without having to purchase devices. Instead, a document solution is designed for the customer, with minimal reliance on hard copy, by using document management software for receiving, storing and transmitting documents digitally. The integrated solution is supported by a maintenance contract that enables devices to be remotely monitored and quickly returned to service if faults occur, further reducing the number of devices needed to support productivity. Managed print is a well-established example of a product-service system and has the added benefit of returning the hardware to the supplier at the end of the contract, to facilitate re-use of products and parts.

Filling a gap in materials recovery with new technology

Carpets are one of the hardest waste streams to recycle, and an estimated half a million tonnes are discarded in the UK every year. Mid UK Recycling (**www.midukrecycling.co.uk/**) developed technology to separate the synthetic fibres in carpets, recovering polypropylene and polyurethane foam. This filled a gap in the processing technology for a waste that would otherwise go to landfill, enabling the company to charge local authorities for processing at a rate equal to landfill charges (the only other option), as well as sell on the recovered materials, giving a double income stream.

Window-maker Veka (**www.veka-recycling.co.uk/index**), a German company, saw the reputational benefits of recycling its PVC window frames. PVC is a very durable plastic – windows have a lifetime of 30–40 years and can be recycled up to ten times, making this a highly resource-efficient use of plastic. Veka bought a UK start-up that had developed the technology to turn discarded windows back into high quality PVC, enabling Veka to feed it back into its windows, thus 'closing the loop' rather than using the materials for lower-grade products. Over a six-year period the company has developed collection methods and processing to the extent that it now supplies a range of other companies with its PVC pellets (which can be turned into any product). With supply and demand now on a stable basis, the biggest threat to expansion of the business is the contamination of the recovered material with other materials. This includes an emerging trend of using strips of glass/plastic composite to make drilling into the windows easier, but which ruins the recycling operation. This is a good example of the design process needing a stimulus from further down the supply chain to 'think circular'.

With innovation, almost anything can be put back into the system. Engineering consultancy Resons Solutions (**http://link2energy.co.uk/ wp-content/uploads/2014/04/Resons-Solutions-Case-Study-Inerts-Fines.pdf**) offers a 'waste to product' service which transforms discarded resources back into valuable products. 'Trommel fines' are one example. This is the material left behind when waste materials are sorted and sieved – it is largely soil, but often has fragments of paper, wood and metal, and would normally be landfilled. Resons have transformed this material into a construction product, ensuring that 100 percent of the material is recycled and diverted from landfill, while still meeting quality protocols set by WRAP. The same can be done with the material from gulley emptying and road sweeping.

The need for analysis

One of the keys to more circular business models is finding ways to guarantee the quality of recovered materials, while making sure that any rules governing 'waste' products are adhered to. This presents many opportunities for companies with analytical capabilities, such as Environmental Scientifics Group (**www.esg.co.uk/case-studies/**). Originally part of a public body and set up to test the quality of coal, the company now provides a wide range of assurance and compliance services that enable 'waste' products to go back into productive use, while making sure that there are no adverse environmental side-effects of that utilisation.

3. **Innovation stimulus**

These are examples of new areas of technology and service provision.

The emerging bio-based economy

The bio-based economy, or bioeconomy, shares goals with the circular economy, in terms of promoting the most efficient use of resources, circulating products for as long as possible, and providing future security of supply for key materials. It is also one of the areas with huge scope for innovation because of advances in chemistry and biology.

New technology is beginning to enable us to do more with organic waste and organic by-products, including 'bio refining', which uses a combination of novel techniques to maximise the use of biomass such as sugars, cellulose and lignin for the efficient extraction of chemicals and proteins. These can then be used at platforms for new and existing fuels, chemicals and materials. As an example, pot ale, a by-product of whisky distilling is worth about £50/tonne. Using a refinery to extract proteins in this whisky by-product produces a product which can be used as food in fish farms, and is worth £1500 per tonne. This is being developed by Horizons Proteins (**http://horizonproteins.com/**) at Heriot-Watt University in Scotland as a commercial spin-off of their research.

The most exciting new developments involve using bio-based materials, including wastes, to replace fossil oil in products such as high-value, specialist chemicals, pharmaceuticals and plastics. The UK is a centre of excellence for many of these strands of work, including research at the University of York (**www.york.ac.uk/news-and-events/news/2014/biohub-funding/**). UK private equity investment company Sinvestec (**www.sinvestec.com/**) specialises in supporting these emerging technologies and helping them to market. The Port of Rotterdam (**www.portofrotterdam.com/nl/actueel/Documents/12.0474%20 CircularEconomy_pdf%20V07.pdf**) is positioning itself as a natural hub for a range of circular models, for bio-based materials as well as metals and oil and gas infrastructure.

Modularity is the way forward for electronics

An important circular economy strategy is upgrading as an alternative to buying a whole new product. Several companies are working on modular mobile phones. Chinese company ZTE (**www.cnet.com/uk/products/zte-eco-mobius-modular-concept-phone/**) says of its concept: 'ECO-MOBIUS allows people to customize or upgrade their mobile phones more cheaply. More importantly, it is a highly efficient component exchange mechanism, making the most of materials and reducing waste.' There is also Google's Project Ara (**www.projectara.com/prize/**), a competition to design novel modules for a smartphone. The success of these concepts will depend on how old modules are recovered and re-used, and their value maximised.

Design for disassembly will be in demand

As both countries and companies show greater ambition in their recycling targets, this will become an important business strategy. Design for disassembly deploys simple design principles such as reducing the number of different types of materials and parts, screwing or snapping components together rather than gluing, clearly marking the positions of key components, and using detachable leads rather than solder for electronic components. Even labels can be important – putting plastic labels on metal parts should be avoided if they're not critical as they interfere with recycling. Electronics company Hewlett Packard (www8. hp.com/us/en/hp-information/environment/design-for-environment. html#.VHjpYFesVUO) uses several of these strategies, and places an environmental steward on every design team to identify design changes that may reduce environmental impact throughout the product's life cycle.

The University of Loughborough (**http://ecodesign.lboro.ac.uk/?section =97**) site has an ecodesign guide, pointing to the clever technologies on the way. They include screws that drop out when slightly heated, or smart barcodes that enable components to be identified and separated. For further detail, see 'The flat screen (LCD) TV: Not designed for recycling' on p. 21 of Green Alliance's 'Reinventing the Wheel' (**www.green-alliance. org.uk/page_77.php**).

Recovered materials ('upcycling') can have their own marketable identity

Rotterdam-based architects Superuse (**http://superuse-studios.com/ index.php/about/**) use recovered materials and products as the starting point for their innovative urban designs, providing something unique for every customer, avoiding waste, and making a virtue of the diversity of materials that come their way.

UK firm Elvis and Kresse (**http://elvisandkresse.com/about/**) takes waste streams that are difficult to reprocess and applies design genius to provide a re-use option. Examples include fire hoses turned into designer handbags, reclaimed leather turned into rugs and bedding turned into industrial textiles.

4. Avoided risk

There are many examples where resource recovery or material avoidance helps to address business risk.

TABLE 2. Some examples of supply chain of risk

MATERIAL AND TYPE OF RISK	ISSUE	CONSEQUENCE
Price risk:		
Copper	Decreasing ore grade means more energy and water needed to mine – a new copper mine in Chile (under severe water pressure) costs twice as much as a decade ago.	Increased prices of copper and other metals; increasing water scarcity leading ultimately to production disruption.
Aluminium	Very high carbon footprint	If carbon were priced according to some recommendations, the price could rise by 70%.

MATERIAL AND TYPE OF RISK	ISSUE	CONSEQUENCE
Political risk:		
Rare earth minerals	Not rare at all, but mining is concentrated in a few countries, and the Chinese tried (successfully) to impose export restrictions to save the metals for their own use, creating uncertainy for companies.	Price rises, limited access to the materials. But likely to stimulate the opening or re-opening of alternative sources.
Nickel	Indonesian government banned export of the ore in 2014	Temporary price rise of more than 50% and continued uncertainty.
Reputational risk:		
Coltan	Mined in the Congo, and the trade used to fund the civil war, leading to Coltan being dubbed a 'Conflict Mineral'.	Consumer boycotts; the Dodd-Frank Act in the USA requiring companies to monitor their supply chains.
Tin	Tin mined in a sensitive area in Indonesia was identified as leading to social and environmental harms by Friends of the Earth.	Large public campaign pressuring users such as Samsung, Apple and others to change their source of supply.

MATERIAL AND TYPE OF RISK	ISSUE	CONSEQUENCE
Palm oil	Identified by campaigning groups as contributing to forest destruction and decline of orangutans	Pressure on manufacturers to use only 'sustainable' sources of palm oil, which costs a third more.
Coal	Coal's contribution to climate change recognised with a 'risk premium' on the financing of new coal power stations in Australia.	Price of new coal power generation raised by 60% making it more expensive than wind power.
Aluminium	One company's disregard for land users and environmental regulations for bauxite mining in India became public through its court actions to challenge the rights of indigenous groups.	Divestments by institutional investors, downgrading of credit rating, calls for delisting from London Stock Exchange, delays in opening the mine led to a refinery being closed.

The circular economy helps to mitigate these risks by fostering an in-depth understanding of the supply chain and where its main impacts lie, and then developing strategies for making better use of the resources by keeping them in the economy for longer. This means lower dependence on risky virgin materials, and gives better control over the future cost base.

These issues are fast climbing the corporate agenda: in a recent PWC survey (**www.pwc.com/gx/en/sustainability/ceo-views/sustainability-perspective.jhtml**) of CEOs, nearly half the respondents put resource scarcity and climate change in their top three 'megatrends', and more than half were concerned about high or volatile raw material costs.

Carbon – it's about the price ...

Analysis by the Carbon Disclosure Project (**https://www.cdp.net/cdpresults/global-price-on-carbon-report-2014.pdf**) reveals that many big businesses are preparing for future regulations requiring greenhouse gas emissions to be priced.

and profitability:

Research by the Carbon Disclosure Project (**https://www.cdp.net/CDPResults/CDP-SP500-leaders-report-2014.pdf**) also found that companies that scored well on disclosing and addressing carbon risks were associated with a significantly higher return on equity than their peers.

... but it's also about the viability of whole countries:

In a report in May 2014, ratings agency Standard and Poor's (S&P) said that climate change will be the 21st century's second global 'mega-trend', after ageing populations, to put downward pressure on sovereign ratings, which could harm economic growth and government coffers. S&P ranked the 116 countries it rates for climate vulnerability, with all of the 20 most vulnerable in emerging markets. Cambodia, Vietnam and Bangladesh occupied the bottom three spots. 'Their vulnerability is in part due to their reliance on agricultural production and employment, which can be vulnerable to shifting climate patterns and extreme weather events, but also due to their weaker capacity to absorb the financial cost' (Reuters report – www.reuters.com/article/2014/05/16/us-credit-climate-idUSKBN0DW15H20140516).

FIGURE 4. Recycling a mobile phone only reduces some of the CO_2 impact of component materials – re-use is better.

Weight of component
materials 100g

Weight of the CO2e embedded in
component materials 200g

Using recycled materials reduces
total CO2e to 100g

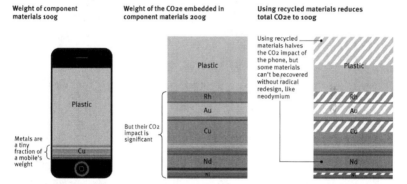

Metals are a tiny fraction of a mobile's weight

But their CO2 impact is significant

Using recycled materials halves the CO2 impact of the phone, but some materials can't be recovered without radical redesign, like neodymium

Plastic
Rh
Au
Cu
Nd
Ni

SOURCE: Green Alliance

5. Brand advantage

This is turning around the risk agenda to show that leading brands are ahead of the pack in understanding their supply chains and addressing challenges.

M&S and 'Shwopping'

The British retailer's campaign has dual aims – to meet equally high profile environmental goals (its Plan A programme) and to raise money for charity. The retailer encourages customers to bring unwanted clothes back to its stores, which are passed on to Oxfam to sell either in stores, in the lucrative international second-hand clothing market or recycled as fibre. The scheme captures people who would not bother to take their clothes to a charity shop but will bring them to M&S (16 items of clothing per person, most of them wearable, are estimated to end up in landfill every year). So far 7.8 million clothes have been brought back, worth £5.5 million to Oxfam. M&S's stated goal (**http://corporate. marksandspencer.com/plan-a/about-plan-a/shwopping**) is to 'collect as many clothes as we sell every year (350 million) and change the way we all shop forever'.

Flooring company Interface (**www.interfaceflor.co.uk/web/Products/ biosfera**) is using nylon from discarded fishing nets, and polymers from recovered cars, in flooring products which can largely be recycled again. The company has made substantial investments in research and technology that will enable these innovations, which have been justified by keeping Interface in the forefront of companies seen to be leading on the environmental and circular economy agendas.

6. A natural progression of the CSR agenda

It is fair to say that the benefits of circular economy approaches are not always easy to quantify, and need to be presented as a package. So for instance, a particular 'circular' project may have a positive but modest return on investment, but might also diversify the supply chain from unquantified but potentially significant risks, and create a marketing opportunity. Together these benefits mean it's more useful than a simple return on investment (ROI) calculation suggests, and a comparison to energy efficiency will be useful here – the immediate savings might not be huge in the scheme of things, but it is the right direction to go for the future.

This sense of a 'right direction' for the future, and being in touch with consumers' desires to avoid waste where possible, is what has led many companies to explore the concept of the circular economy. They often see it as a part of a larger CSR agenda, of stewardship of natural resources, addressing climate change, and safeguarding water and natural areas. They recognise the inter-related nature of these issues, as well as the public concerns associated with them, and look for ways to play their part in improvement. Where these values are espoused by large companies with extensive supply chains, it is only a matter of time before they look to their suppliers to help meet their goals, and drive progress by setting new procurement standards for suppliers.

The John Lewis Partnership, a company with a high reputation for social responsibility, joined forces with a plastics recycler to ensure that as much of its plastic waste as possible was used in the UK. 'We want to be completely transparent in our approach to waste management and ensure that as much as possible is recycled and then reused in our own businesses', according to Mike Walters, Recycling and Waste Operations Manager for the John Lewis Partnership:

By working with Centriforce (**www.centriforce.com/en/news/john-lewis-partnership-aims-closed-loop-new-waste-plastics-strategy/**), the John Lewis Partnership can ensure it avoids landfill costs and makes an income from its waste arisings. Furthermore, it is pioneering closed loop arrangements which provide the perfect demonstration of total waste ownership as well as underpinning the company's sustainable corporate responsibility.

Chapter recap

Here are the reasons for exploring more 'circular' approaches that you might deploy in discussion with colleagues:

- **Economic resilience** as a reason can be seen in companies such as **Unilever** and **British Telecom**.

- **New business opportunities** are seen in the development of **new recycling technologies**, the growing number of companies looking at **leasing models** for appliances and clothes, and the development of companies who can offer the right kind of **analysis** and **assurance** of recovered products and materials.

- **Innovation stimulus** is clear for companies involved in the **bio-economy, novel forms of re-use, modular design** and **design for disassembly.**

- **Risk avoidance** is crucial for supply chains that may raise **reputational issues**, or have high embedded carbon and be vulnerable to carbon pricing, or rely on supply chains involving countries economically vulnerable to **climate change impacts** or **niche materials.**

- **Brand advantage** on circular economy has worked for **Marks and Spencer, Kyocera** and **Interface**.

- **Circular thinking** is a natural extension of the CSR agenda, evidenced by companies such as the **John Lewis Partnership**.

STEP 3

Reviewing Your Organisation's Potential for Implementing More Circular Approaches

SO NOW YOU HAVE BUY-IN from colleagues in your business for starting to 'think circular'. Where do you begin?

Look at your business

Circular economy approaches are relevant to you wherever you are in the supply chain – primary extraction, manufacturing, transport and logistics, retail, recovery. The next important step is to work out where in your business they might have most benefit. Use Table 3 to identify the relevance to your business.

TABLE 3. Summary of benefits from circular economy approaches

Type of benefit	Applies if	Possible scale	Examples
Savings on raw materials from internal recycling	You use raw materials	Small to very large	Metals

Type of benefit	Applies if	Possible scale	Examples
Savings on raw materials from recovering used products	You use raw materials or complex components	Medium to very large	Car parts, electronics; Metals, plastics
Developing re-use as a business opportunity	You have or can organise storage facilities, have good logistics links, and access to reasonably high value products	Medium to very large	Furniture, shop fittings, home appliances, phones, games, clothes
Remanu-facturing opportunities	You make or import a complex product where the components have materials of interest but would be costly to disassemble	Medium to large	Engines, motors, photo-copiers, printer cartridges
Mutually beneficial supply chain collaborations	You are anywhere in the supply chain	Small to very large	Packaging reprocessing, equipment sharing
Getting value from organic wastes	You generate organic wastes	Medium to very large	Energy from anaerobic digestion; providing feedstock for biorefineries

Type of benefit	Applies if	Possible scale	Examples
Innovation stimulus	Any	Any	New uses for materials, new design for modularity, dissassembly
Risk avoidance	Any, but particularly with long supply chains involving emerging economies	Any	Reputational risks from poor land use practices, use of conflict minerals
Brand advantage	Any, but particularly consumer-facing	Any, but particularly large – more to lose	Demonstrating resource stewardship, local sourcing and recycling
CSR extension	Any	Any, but particularly large	Demonstrating global respon-sibility for multinational companies

Circular approaches are particularly beneficial for supply chains involving:

Construction products

A lot of material is involved in building. High-value, high environmental impact materials such as steel and aluminium are often embedded in lower value materials such as concrete, so that they are difficult to reclaim without turning them into scrap – for instance, steel building girders. This points to the need for better design, in both buildings and materials.

FIGURE 5. London's Olympic stadium was built with reused oil pipelines, saving the energy required to recycle the steel

SOURCE: CC-BY Wikipedia user BaldBoris

Automotive

This sector also uses a lot of material, some of it of high value, as well as complex valuable components such as engines, motors and the magnets in electric cars. 'Circular' systems already work well in the automotive industry in Europe, thanks to specific regulations requiring recovery of materials, but could still be improved.

Metal products

These are always worth keeping in use as long as possible, and keeping in as close to their original state, as avoiding remelting avoids loss of materials and energy. For instance, even though aluminium is easily recyclable, and has very high environmental impact because of the energy and water used to make it, we only manage to recycle about half of it worldwide because we use it in short-lived products such as cans, which we fail to recover.

Electronics and household appliances

The complexity and multi-material nature of electronics mean that recycling the materials recovers much less value than re-using or remanufacturing. This is true for any product with complex design, multi-material components and meant to last for months or years. Work done by Green Alliance shows that for mobile phones, the value recovered from a broken iPhone, when repaired, is about a third of its original value (£170); whereas the value recovered by recycling is about one quarter of 1 percent, or about 75p.

Textiles

Textiles are the hardest material category to recycle because of their mix of fibres and the energy and water required to turn recovered fibres back into usable product. This makes longer life, re-use and refurbishment very much the preferred option.

Packaging

This is the opposite of products like electronics – it fulfils an important function protecting products (for instance, preventing food waste), but is generally short-lived and bulky, making transportation of recovered materials expensive. Here the future emphasis might be on 'bioeconomy' solutions such as packaging materials that can be composted. This is particularly important where the packaging is likely to be mixed up with food waste (e.g. clingfilm), marrying up recovery with that of the food waste. It is also important to establish 'reverse logistics' systems for the more valuable packaging materials such as rigid plastics and metals that can be easily reused, or at least cleaned and recycled.

The different circular economy strategies for different types of product are shown in Table 4.

TABLE 4. How the circular economy strategies divide up
(with thanks to James Walker, Kingfisher)

COMPLEX, SHORT-LIVED, e.g.	SIMPLE, SHORT-LIVED, e.g.
• Electronics • Printer cartridges **Strategies:** 1st: Re-use, refurbish, remanufacture 2nd: Recover materials	• Packaging **Strategies:** 1st: Re-use (particularly business to business packaging, e.g. trays and pallets) 2nd: Recover materials, compost
COMPLEX, LONG-LIVED, e.g.	SIMPLE, LONG-LIVED, e.g.
• Cars • Washing machines • Fridges **Strategies:** 1st: Improve longevity, offer service options 2nd: Re-use, refurbish, remanufacture 3rd: Recover materials	• Textiles from pure fibres • Furniture mainly made from one material • Construction materials **Strategies:** 1st: Improve longevity, offer service options 2nd: Re-use, refurbish 3rd: Recover materials

Look at your values

It is important to be clear about values and potential for change within your organisation:

- Is incremental change the existing, and only likely, model?

- Is there the possibility of disruptive innovation or radical change?

- Is talk of 'new business models' a pipe dream or a strong possibility?

- Does the idea of a 'roadmap' have meaning within your business, or do you have some other expression of wanting to get from where you are now, to a different set of future activities?

- How important is backing from key individuals, or an 'evidence base' or external funding? How would you go about assembling all of these?

Talking through these options with colleagues will help to identify the art of the possible – gradual steps, or radical changes. We recommend considering systematically:

What you can do within your business

Buildings – can you refurbish rather than building new? Ensure that any new construction or refurbishment meets 'circular', that is, material recovery objectives. Where have the materials come from? Are there any reputational issues associated with them? Can you re-use components from other buildings? Do the materials have recycled content? Can they be easily separated and reclaimed at the end of the building's life?

Product design – if you are a designer, or a specifier for design, have you ensured that the design process takes account of the sources of the raw materials, how efficiently they are used, and how they can be reclaimed at end of life? And how the product can have maximum longevity for its function? For more on this, see the forthcoming Dō Short from The Great Recovery Project.

Production efficiency – if you are a manufacturer, have you analysed all opportunities for getting more product out of fewer raw materials? Is all scrap recycled internally? If this is not possible with existing processes, what would have to change and what would it cost to make it possible?

Logistics – if you move goods around, have you explored all possibilities for 'reverse logistics' where you take recovered materials back after delivering new goods?

Service options – could you offer a service instead of the actual product, for example, use of tyres by mileage needed rather than selling the tyres, leasing of carpets, redecoration instead of selling paint. Service options could be allied with setting up repair, refurbishment or remanufacturing operations in order to improve the economics.

Where you can influence others

If you are a 'business to business' buyer of materials or components, have you identified the parts of your supply chain that might raise concerns, or where you could influence greater recovery, or the use of more recovered content? Have you explored the product design, production efficiency and logistics points above with the main players in your supply chains?

If you are in retail, and have control over the way the things you sell are made, have you explored all design and specification avenues for improving recovery, as in the bullet point above?

If you are in the materials recovery business, have you taken steps to understand the materials flows of the businesses in your area? What are they generating, what could be used by others, what might have local markets and what might have wider markets? Is collection cost a barrier for them to having more material recovered (as against sending it to landfill), and if so, could you foster collaborations that share these costs?

Do you need independent brokers as a 'matchmaking' service? If so, it may be that WRAP or other local organisations could help.

Going further, **could you enter into joint ventures with companies in your supply chain**, or maybe outside, to put in place the right infrastructure to get recovery of products or materials, and ensure a steady supply?

Could you engage in 'pre-competitive' contact with similar companies to work out how you might collaborate?

This last point, on 'pre-competitive' behaviour, is tricky. Competition law dictates that companies should not collaborate in any way that might result in price-fixing, so many companies are understandably nervous about these kind of discussions. This issue arose when WRAP was holding talks with companies about how far they could set targets for waste reduction. However, examination by WRAP's legal team concluded that the danger of conflicting with competition law was more a perception than a reality, and companies can go further than they think towards agreeing issues such as what is a realistic recovery target in the sector for certain materials, and sharing information on best practice. A neutral host such as WRAP, or a trade association, can help to reassure companies that they are the right side of the law. Nonetheless, this issue does need clarifying, something that Green Alliance is working on with the government. WRAP can also advise on current practice.

Where you can disrupt others

The circular economy will need to reflect the way the economy works now – not all companies have the appetite or culture to collaborate. A more radical option is to identify where your company can outcompete someone in your supply chain. Examples of this include B&Q developing a leasing model for more durable power tools. Most consumers don't need to own tools, they just want to use them for a few DIY projects – leasing creates the opportunity for more profit for B&Q while reducing the sales of manufacturers making cheap tools. Of course, there's nothing to stop manufacturers from setting up their own leasing systems!

Where you probably need collaboration

- Getting access to detailed product information.

- Gaining a detailed understanding of 'end of life' (perhaps more accurately end of first life) or 'circular' options for all products (particularly novel materials and products). This represents a big data task, and beyond the reach of many SMEs. This is a case for government support and/or input from brands who are likely to gain from having such information.

- Getting agreement across a whole sector, which is an opportunity for trade bodies or even the government, through bodies like WRAP or via the UK government's industrial strategy.

- Setting up systems that require economies of scale, or where there is a large and risky investment in new processes, for example, some recycling innovations that would benefit from risk sharing across several businesses.

Identifying barriers

The barriers you are likely to come across are:

Internal

- Lack of senior management commitment.

- Lack of time to consider the possibilities.

- Not factoring in material risks to business decisions.

- Lack of understanding of the principles of the circular economy.

- Not accepting the data on benefits, or not feeling that they are large enough in proportion to the effort, or in proportion to the company's activities.

- Not being prepared to accept a long enough return on investment.

- Sunk costs in old infrastructure.

- Perceived uncertainty about future policy or regulation, leading to inertia.

- Lack of technical expertise on new process options.

External

- Poor design of products in your supply chain, making separation and recovery more challenging.

- Lack of leadership from the government or from the heavyweight players in your sector.

- Encountering resistance from your supply chain (due to factors above).

- Not having quite enough control over the crucial bits of the supply chain.

- Lack of recovery and reprocessing infrastructure.

- Split incentives – the benefits of new infrastructure accrue to people other than those being asked to pay for them.

- Not finding appropriate partners.

- Not finding anyone who can act as intermediary.

- Lack of contract expertise to make new kinds of deals.

The first step is to work out which of these barriers are in play.

For internal barriers, the quickest route might be hold a workshop or strategy day on 'the meaning of the circular economy'. This might be suggested on the basis that:

- It is a new buzz-word – the company needs to decide if it has any substance or relevance.

- It has some interesting people behind it (Caterpillar, Renault, National Grid, Interface, Ellen MacArthur et al.).

- There is evidence that it can save a lot of money.

- Diversifying your business makes sense via service models or away from risky raw materials.

And also perhaps:

- Other businesses in the supply chain are asking about it (B2B has been the most fertile ground for many current examples of circular economy).

- Customers are asking about it.

If a workshop is too much of a step initially, a briefing paper could be commissioned. This might later feed into a workshop. The paper could use this book to provide a summary of issues.

The briefing paper or event would need to consider a worked example to help to identify barriers and solutions. For instance, someone might have asked 'how efficient will our new buildings/office refurbishment/ furniture/product line be' which provides a hook to explore circular options.

What are the consumer trends? The rise of iFixit

The website iFixit.com features repair manuals for an increasing number of consumer products, including cars, cameras, smartphones, washing machines and other household appliances. The home page declares: 'You bought it, you should own it. Period. You should have the right to use it, modify it, and repair it wherever, whenever, and however you want. Defend your right to fix.' These sentiments are representative of a consumer base increasingly disgruntled by expensive products that are not amenable to repair. iFixit's customer survey (**http://ifixit.org/blog/4631/ifixit-community-survey-the-results-are-in/**) showed that 95 percent of iFixit users would be more likely to buy from a company whose product they've successfully repaired.

Finding solutions

There is no 'one size fits all' answer to the barriers, but here is how some of the examples we have encountered have tackled the problems:

Internal

Barrier: Lack of time to consider the possibilities.

Solution: If 'moving towards the circular economy' can attract board interest, this can be translated into asking for briefings and options, which in itself mandates the time needed to make at least an initial investigation.

Barrier: Not factoring material risks and supply chain risks into business decisions.

Solution: It is good practice to consider material risks on a company's risk register – you could approach the chair of your audit and risk committee (if there is one) or the board member responsible for risk, to ask if this has been done or could be done. If it is done in a less formal way, find out which company personnel are involved, and ask them to give a briefing on their current approach to material risks.

Barrier: Lack of understanding of the principles of the circular economy.

Solution: This is where careful briefing comes in, drawing on this book, and the work of the Ellen MacArthur Foundation, WRAP, Green Alliance and others.

Barrier: Not accepting the data on benefits, or feeling that they are not large enough in proportion to the effort, or in proportion to the company's activities.

Solution: Taking the case study examples in Step 2 above, can you make an initial assessment of what might be the benefits of adopting similar approaches? You need to argue that there are multiple benefits, and long-term benefits – not just monetary savings, but greater resilience (through having more control over the supply chain) and also reputational benefits. The benefits of gaining a better understanding of the supply chain are numerous.

Barrier: Not being prepared to accept a long enough return on investment.

Solution: This is one of the hardest barriers – examples are needed of successful companies in your sector who have accepted longer ROI, possibly due to different cultures in other countries. In the end, however, this is about banks and shareholders' attitudes. Wherever possible, ensure that they are briefed as well.

Barrier: Sunk costs in old infrastructure.

Solution: It is worth working out if these could be re-purposed in any way, or ascertaining how soon they are likely to be written off.

Barrier: Perceived uncertainty about future policy or regulation, leading to inertia.

Solution: This will always be the case, but competitive businesses stay ahead or at least abreast of these changes. Any initiatives that improve recovery of resources are unlikely to be out of step with policy developments, and it is possible that government action will catch up with 'first movers' to create a level playing field.

Barrier: Lack of technical expertise on material recovery process options.

Solution: This is a developing field so expertise should become available, but it is also worth considering how trainee schemes can take on board the issues, and perhaps partnering with academic institutions could bring in new skills and innovative thinking. It's also worth getting in touch with Innovate UK (formerly the Technology Strategy Board or TSB; **https://www.gov.uk/government/organisations/innovate-uk**) which may be able to help fund commercialisation of innovative, circular economy processes. There are a growing number of specialist consultants – try the ENDS Directory (**https://www.endsdirectory.com/**).

External

Barrier: Lack of appreciation of the benefits of using recovered materials.

Solution: This is a case of pointing out the cost, risk avoidance and brand advantages of recovered materials. Use examples like Coca Cola, Marks & Spencer and John Lewis, in Chapter 2 above.

Barrier: Poor design of products, making separation and recovery more challenging.

Solution: As well as looking at redesigning your own products, where relevant, look for opportunities to flex supply chain muscle, or work with other companies in your sector to get enough critical mass to challenge the design decisions of those supplying products to you.

Barrier: Lack of leadership from the government or from the heavyweight players in your sector.

Solution: This is a case of lobbying government and leading business institutions.

Barrier: Encountering resistance from your supply chain

Solution: This demands working closely and collaboratively with supply chain companies to overcome obstacles and identify the benefits to be achieved. Again, WRAP can help through its voluntary agreements.

Barrier: Not having quite enough control over the crucial bits of the supply chain.

Solution: Here again collaboration is the name of the game – strategic alliances that transcend completion but offer more supply chain clout. If that is not feasible, it may be that creating a competitor company, and disrupting the supply chain, is better value in the longer term.

Barrier: Lack of recovery and reprocessing infrastructure.

Solution: This is where the strategic alliances aim to actually put kit on the ground. Coca Cola's joint venture with Eco-plastics to build a bottle-to-bottle plastics recycling plant, and to buy the products from the plant, is a good example of a strategic alliance.

Barrier: Split incentives – the benefits of new infrastructure accrue to people other than those being asked to pay for them.
Solution: As above, what is the deal that will put kit on the ground, and offer some return to all involved?

Barrier: Not finding appropriate partners.
Solution: Business organisations such as trade associations and professional bodies need to gear up to help provide contacts.

Barrier: Not finding anyone who can act as intermediary.
Solution: WRAP is one of the organisations best equipped to do this, as well as the Centre for Remanufacturing and Reuse. The Ellen MacArthur Foundation and Aldersgate Group can also provide support. See the list of resources in the last chapter.

Barrier: Lack of contract expertise to make new kinds of deals.
Solution: The role of business advisers needs to be boosted to bring in more 'circular economy' contracting expertise – this might be a role for trade associations.

Keeping an eye on the system level

The above list of suggestions for overcoming internal and external barriers shows that there is a lot that individual companies can do to kick-start the circular economy. But we must not lose sight of the fact that the circular economy is a system – everything needs to work together to deliver better resource management. Figure 6 is the ideal situation.

....

FIGURE 6. The virtuous triangle for the circular economy.

Companies develop
new business models
and design for recovery

Recovery infrastructure
is built to capture value
from old products

Customers demand
lower impact, circular
products

....

The stimulus for this can come from a number of directions, but stimulus is certainly needed to break out of the dominant economic and social behaviours that keep us in largely linear mode.

Many of these stimuli can come from companies themselves:

- developing new models such as access to products rather than ownership

- redesigning products for easier re-use and recovery

- collaboration through the supply chain for better recovery

- making circular behaviour part of the brand.

But some are harder for businesses alone to deliver:

- design standards that create a level playing field

- targets and incentives that encourage businesses and consumers to take advantage of recycling systems

- investment in reprocessing plants that can only work at large scale, and are therefore large and potentially risky investments

- fiscal incentives that will make secondary materials more cost-effective than primary.

It is important for companies to form a view as to what kinds of external stimuli will best help them to evolve new, circular business models. This is itself a somewhat 'circular' process as, for most governments, strong business support is key to developing and successfully delivering new policies, just as an intelligent government framework is key to businesses delivering their end of the circular economy.

Green Alliance has forged a coalition of businesses, The Circular Economy Task Force (**www.green-alliance.org.uk/CETF.php**), to make recommendations to government on how it can support the circular economy.

The EEF (**www.eef.org.uk/releases/uk/2014/Government-warned-to-act-over-growing-risk-to-material-supply-as-UK-approaches-end-of-an-era.htm**), the organisation for those involved in manufacturing businesses, has made an in-depth analysis of the material risks facing companies, and recommendations for how government policy can help.

Chapter recap

- **Look at your business** – What sector? Which products? Which services? How big? Where does your supply change reach?

- **Look at your values** – Incremental change? Radical change?

- **What you can do within your business** – Start with construction, product design, reverse logistics and recovery options.

- **Where you can influence others** – Procurement and specification.

- **Where you can disrupt others** – Whose market could you take with more circular approaches?

- **Where you probably need collaboration** – Getting scale and clout through getting the supply chain to work together.

- **Identifying barriers** – Internal and external.

- **Finding solutions** – There are organisations to help.

- **Don't forget the system level** – What do you need from government policy?

STEP 4

Identifying Priorities and Measuring Success

Some approaches to indicators

THERE IS A BEWILDERING ARRAY of 'metrics' and 'indicators' in play that relate to circular economy goals. These have come forward from governments, multi-national institutions, consultants, businesses, NGOs and others, and reflect different goals and world-views about what is important. We'd suggest that the outcomes that the circular economy helps create are the most important thing to measure: the amount of desirable materials saved, the money earned, and the carbon emissions (or water) avoided.

Many businesses find that relative metrics are the more useful indicators – money saved as a proportion of turnover, or carbon saved as a proportion of total carbon emissions in a year, or even carbon saved compared to the growth in the business. These are the kind of indicators that can most easily be turned into forward **targets**, because you know exactly what you are seeking to change. Then you would need to decide whether these metrics, indicators and targets remain **internal** – that is, they are for the information and motivation of those inside the company; or if they are to be used for **external** purposes, and thus become part of corporate reporting on company performance, or are aimed at helping consumers make decisions.

No indicator or metric will fully capture how 'circular' a country, business or product really is, but some offer more promise than others in terms of aiding understanding of whether progress is being made. Below is a summary of the most useful.

Material flow analyses (MFA)

For: Geographical areas like a country or region; economic units like a company.

Aim: To track the flow of materials within a given system on the basis of weight. They can track 'circularity' by showing the proportion of primary raw material input to secondary (recovered) raw material, if the data are available.

Examples: Julian Allwood et al.'s diagrams of global flows of key materials (**www.lcmp.eng.cam.ac.uk/wp-content/uploads/T2-Report-web.pdf**). WRAP's sankey diagrams of materials flows in the UK (**www.wrap.org. uk/content/material-flows-uk**). Biffa's mass balance reports on whole regions and sectors (**http://centrallobby.politicshome.com/Resources/ epolitix/Forum%20Microsites/Biffa%20Waste%20Services%20Ltd/ Biffaward%20Programme%20on%20Sustainable%20Resource%20 Use.113.pdf**).

Strengths: Give a broad-brush picture of major flows and how much is being recovered, which can help set priorities, and, depending on how often data are gathered, can show changes over time.

Weaknesses: For countries, data are derived from national statistics which can only measure material types (e.g. 'metals' or 'biomass') rather than individual materials. Weight alone does not capture the environmental impacts of different materials, so the picture is incomplete. Most analyses exclude water, as the relative weight would distort the picture.

There are variants of Material Flow Analysis used in national statistics. *Domestic Material Consumption* measures the materials used in an economy, both what is generated in the country and what comes in from abroad. It has robust data, and can be compared with GDP, so it can show efficiencies over time (i.e. reducing material consumption per unit of GDP over a number of years). But it doesn't look at what is cycled within the economy so it is not very useful for assessing circularity. Similarly, *Raw Material Consumption and Total Material Consumption*, capture different scopes of consumption, but don't always capture recovery.

The most immediately useful indicator is probably *Environmentally-weighted Material Consumption (EMC)*, which builds on materials use data already collected by many companies and the kind of impact factors used for lifecycle analysis.

In the diagram below, the impact chosen is carbon emissions, and shows the benefits of using recovered gold in, for instance, a mobile phone.

....

FIGURE 7. Measuring risk for gold using Environmentally Weighted Material Consumption (EMC)

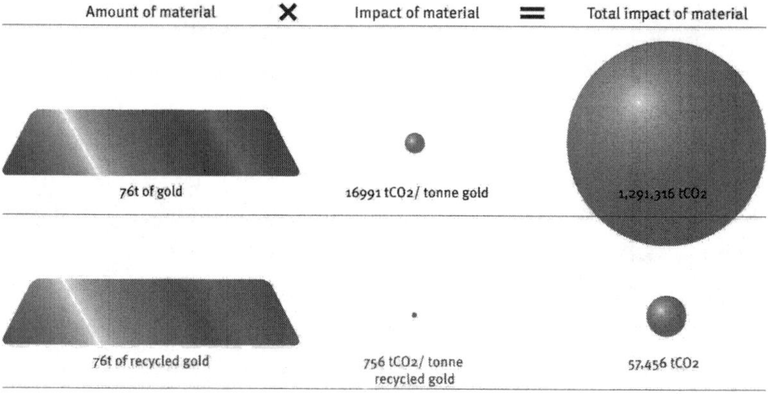

Amount of material	**✗**	Impact of material	**=**	Total impact of material

76t of gold   16991 tCO2/ tonne gold   1,291,316 tCO2

76t of recycled gold   756 tCO2/ tonne recycled gold   57,456 tCO2

SOURCE: Green Alliance

....

Life cycle analysis (LCA)

For: designers, manufacturers and retailers of products; possibly consumers.

Aim: To measure the environmental impact of products by choosing key parameters (carbon emissions, water, waste, toxicity, effects on biodiversity) and measuring where these impacts arise: extraction of raw materials, in the manufacturing process, in use, and at end of life.

Strengths: Good for building up a detailed picture of product impacts, in order to understand where to intervene to best effect. This includes understanding the relative benefits of pursuing circularity strategies such as reusability, remanufacturing and recyclability because aspects like avoided waste of raw materials, and associated carbon emissions and water use can be measured and compared. Gathering these data often has a significant effect on decision-making inside a company, as it provides 'evidence' of impact and proportionality that can be used at all levels of the organisation.

Weaknesses: Very data intensive and therefore expensive. Some companies can afford to do their own analysis, but some have to rely on generic data, which is cheaper but may be out of date, leading to lack of comparability between products. This makes it difficult to use the LCAs as a means of communicating authoritatively with consumers and enabling choice.

There is an effort at EU level to address the shortcomings of LCAs by developing **Product Environmental Footprints**, which would group products into categories to make them easier to handle, and then standardise the LCA methodologies applied. This should give more confidence about the comparability of products, and so be more robust to put in front of consumers, but is a lengthy and detailed task requiring cooperation between a large number of companies, and is still at an early stage.

A potentially easier task is **Environmental Product Declarations**, which seek to report on what the company considers are the most important aspects of environmental impact of the product, but without necessarily obtaining full LCA data. This can be helpful both inside the company and for consumers, but may lay the company open to charges of glossing over the detail (for more, see Ramon Arratia's Dō Short – **www. dosustainability.com/shop/full-product-transparency-p-11.html**).

WRAP's Product Sustainability Forum

The Product Sustainability Forum (PSF) is a collaboration of organisations made up of grocery retailers and suppliers, academics, NGOs and UK Government representatives.

It provides a platform for these organisations to work together to measure, improve and communicate the environmental performance of grocery products. WRAP provides the Secretariat for the forum.

Many companies have already started measuring the environmental performance of products. The PSF was established to lead, co-ordinate and progress existing efforts, alongside similar initiatives being undertaken around the world so that industry, governments and others have evidence to help them prioritise which products to focus their efforts on.

The 2013 report 'An initial assessment of the environmental impact of grocery products' (**www.wrap.org.uk/priorityproducts**), plus a range of practical materials (**www.wrap.org.uk/node/15814**) are designed to help companies implement product improvements.

Boots evaluation tool wins Guardian sustainable business award

The Guardian reported:

> *The Boots Botanics range has 180 products and combines plant extracts with the latest skincare technology. In order to improve its sustainability, Boots analysed the journey of every Botanics product from design to end-of-life, creating more sustainable, ethical sourcing practices as it went along. To make this possible Boots developed a sophisticated evaluation tool. Peer-reviewed by Forum for the Future, the web-based product sustainability assessment (PSA) tool was introduced in 2011. Taking into account 24 criteria, product developers at Boots can build a product profile that allows them to evaluate the performance of individual ingredients, products and entire product ranges.*

The tool was used to set objectives and measure sustainability improvements when the Botanics brand was re-launched in 2012. Boots were able to define measureable improvements in the new product range with an average improvement of over 30 percent in sustainability indices across the brand. This sustained effort at better understanding the impact to its products has enhanced Boot's reputation with a large range of stakeholders.

Kingfisher's 'Closed Loop Calculator' – assessing products in 10 quick questions

Kingfisher's calculator uses 10 questions to measure how 'closed loop' a product is. Criteria include what the product is made from, if it can be rented or repaired and whether it can be disassembled into component parts or materials. The company has determined that a product with 'excellent' closed loop credentials will achieve a rating of above 75 percent and a 'very good' product will rate above 55 percent. (For further information, see Kingfisher's 'The Business Opportunity of Closed Loop Innovation' – **https://www.kingfisher.com/netpositive/files/downloads/kingfisher_closed_loop_innovation.pdf**.)

Circular 'ability' indicators

For: Consumers of products.

Aim: A simple yes/no indicator of whether a product can be recovered or recycled.

Strengths: Relatively simple to communicate once product design has ensured the recyclability of materials, or design for disassembly or design for upgradability, or remanufacturing.

Weaknesses: Doesn't directly indicate actual material use, and therefore also can't indicate actual environmental impact, or the degree to which the product will actually be recycled or otherwise recovered.

Circular use indicators

For: Specific products – consumers and companies.

Aim: To measure actual circular processes for particular products, such as whether a product has recycled content, or reusable bottles are actually reused.

Strengths: More of an indicator of progress than circular 'ability' indicators which only indicate potential. It might be possible to estimate the virgin materials or products displaced by reuse or recycling, and thus have an estimate of environmental impact avoided.

Weaknesses: Complex to establish systems to certify precise amounts of recycled content (it all gets mixed together) or measure specific product re-use.

Japan's pioneering 'Fundamental plan for establishing a sound material cycle society' aims to measure actual circular use (although for the moment only on a weight basis, not environmental impact) and also measure the size of the second hand goods market, and the size of the market for renting and leasing. The plan is underpinned by a series of laws, including requirements for businesses and consumers to separate materials to make recovery easier.

Entropic overhead

This is a new metric in development by consultants hoping to give business Green Alliance es a finer-grained sense of the environmental advantages of 'circular' strategies. Entropy is the loss of energy as materials move through their lifecycle: put simply, it focuses on keeping as much embodied energy in use, and highlights where the scale of collection, reprocessing, or repair significantly affects the amount and quality of energy used across a product's whole lifetime. It can identify where repair might not make sense – for example, when heavy products must be transported over long distances, or where the energy intensity of small-scale repair is greater than the creation of a new, more efficient product. The metric is being developed in consultation with academics and businesses, to test its usefulness and understand what would be involved in gathering the data.

Developments in Europe

Under the Europe 2020 strategy, resource efficiency is identified as one of seven initiatives for 'sustainable growth'. Following the publication of the Resource Efficiency Road Map, the European Commission is consulting on a proposed set of resource efficiency indicators (**http://ec.europa.eu/ environment/consultations/pdf/consultation_resource.pdf**) to monitor progress towards its 2020 target. Given the focus on sustainable growth, the commission proposed a headline indicator of **'resource productivity'** measured as GDP divided by Raw Material Consumption and expressed as euro/tonne (weight of stuff needed to make a given amount of money). This enables a simplistic monitoring of 'decoupling' of economic growth from environmental impact at the nation-state level, but can at least in part take account of imported raw materials.

Beneath this top level indicator, the commission proposed a 'dashboard' of indicators that provide a more detailed picture of resource consumption and associated environmental impacts. Resource consumption and environmental impact indicators are considered in connection to four areas: materials, water, land and energy and climate; and at two scales: domestic and global. Finally, to track policy effectiveness against key thematic areas outlined in the resource efficiency road map, the commission propose a third tier of 'thematic' indicators. These include measures for 'transforming the economy' and 'natural capital and ecosystem services'.

What might work best?

As noted in the gold example in Figure 7, combining the strengths of material flow analysis (understanding what materials are going where) with the strengths of life cycle analysis (what are the impacts of those materials) might yield the best indicators. The formal means of doing this is sometimes called **'environmentally weighted material consumption'**. It applies LCA-derived impact factors (e.g. tonnes of carbon used to create a tonne of steel, for example) and multiplies this by the amount of steel used by a company. By comparing multiple sorts of impact, a material (or product if the approach is applied to all components in a product) can be profiled.

This approach yields **'hotspots'** – it highlights which materials are being used in the largest quantities, cross-referenced with the materials with greatest impact. This is what the European Commission would like to achieve, but doing it for the whole of Europe is an enormous task. For a company, however, such an approach might not be impossible, at least as a broad-brush picture to start with. It subscribes to what is often thought of as the 80/20 rule – find out where the bulk of the problem lies.

The methodology is broadly as shown in Table 5, illustrating a product with varied materials:

TABLE 5. Hotspot analysis

Materials used in the product (in order of quantity used)/ Impacts	Carbon intensity (data for this are available and robust)	Water intensity (data for this are increasingly available, but depends on where the water comes from)	Material risks (these can be difficult to identify without specialist support)	Price or change of price over time (most companies have these data already)
Steel	High	Medium	High (price of some alloys)	High
Aluminium	High	High	Low	High
Bioplastics	Low	High	Low	High
Polymers	Medium	Medium	Medium (price)	Medium
Glass	High	Low	Low	Low
Rare earth metals	Low	Medium	High (access)	High
Lead	Medium	Medium	High (toxicity, reputation)	Medium

This table illustrates how soon subjective judgements on priorities are needed once the data are in. The table suggests that on environmental impact data, plus considering value, the top three materials need attention, to make sure that as much as possible is recovered: preferably by the company concerned, but otherwise by others in the supply chain. After that, there may be choices about priorities, depending on the quantities of materials used, and the detailed assessment of risk – although ultimately the aim should be to get all materials to be circular.

So from that table, likely actions might be:

- Design of the product should be adapted to make sure steel components can be easily recovered and re-used, in a closed loop that the company operates itself. The same with the rare earths.

- The same for aluminium, where re-use is the optimum solution, and new industrial processes are emerging.

- The glass and polymers are not as much of a priority, but in the medium to longer term, strategies such as making them more easily re-usable and recyclable should be considered. They might be substituted with bio-based plastics if the footprint can be shown to be lower.

- The lead should be designed out – there are available substitutes and the toxicity is not worth the reputational risk.

One of the useful aspects of this way of thinking is that, if the data are available, a hotspot analysis can be done by any of the players in the supply chain. Each player might not have the power to alter all or any of the parameters, but the analysis will enable a conversation about who does have power and influence, and may also lead to collaborations that tackle the hotspots.

This was the case with the dairy road map (**www.dairyroadmap.com**/), which involved 25 organisations from across Britain's dairy industry, including farming representatives, manufacturers, retailers and government. Together with work by WRAP, the process identified energy, water and other 'hotspots' for different dairy products, which enabled everyone in the supply chain to set reduction targets.

Free assessment tools

WRAP's Lifetime Optimisation Tool

This tool is designed to answer the question: 'what is the optimum lifetime of your product? Is its best environmental option to be refurbished or to be replaced by a more efficient model? And how long should it be designed to last?'

The Lifetime Optimisation Tool is intended to help retailers, brands, buyers and/or designers understand the 'optimum life' of products and identify where the greatest environmental savings can be made.

By analysing different scenarios, the tool illustrates whether life extension or manufacturing a new product would be more beneficial, and how long a new product should be used to have fewer impacts than the original.

It is free to download from the WRAP website (**www.wrap.org.uk/content/lifetime-optimisation-tool-0**).

Centre for Reuse and Remanufacturing ReOpt Tool

ReOpt is a software tool to help companies decide if their product would be suitable for remanufacturing. It helps assess the nature

---

of the product, customers, markets, environmental factors and the resources used in the product.

It is free to download from the CRR website (**www.remanufacturing. org.uk/remanufacturing-decision-tool.lasso**).

Indicators of high level attention, also known as 'business process indicators'

Sometimes the important indicators are not ones needing material or environmental impact data. They can be measuring the level of attention and action that the company is applying. The most important of these are:

- Appointing a board director with responsibility for the commercial implications of material risk and circular behaviour.

- The detailing of material security issues on company risk registers.

- Discussion of risks with shareholders and investors of the issues facing companies, and rewards from those groups for taking action.

Conclusion

Given the variety of metrics available and breadth of experience already built up in the business world, there is no excuse for failing to put in place some key metrics as part of a company's participation in the circular economy, although it may not be possible to immediately populate them all with data. However, the process helps to identify what information is needed from suppliers, which in turn helps them to put the right systems in place. It may help to convene suppliers at the start of the process to share available information and identify gaps. The overall lesson is that information and expertise is needed from all players to generate robust system-wide indicators of progress.

Lexmark – Setting circular goals

Lexmark (**www.lexmark.com/en_us/products/supplies-and-access ories/collection-and-recycling-program.html**), a US-based global provider of printing and imaging solutions, serves businesses in over 170 countries. The company has reduced its CO_2 emissions by 45 percent since 2005. One of its core resource efficiency targets is to increase the use of post-consumer recycled (PCR) plastic content in its toner cartridges from the present 10 percent to 25 percent by 2018.

Lexmark also has a stated goal to regionally source 80 percent of its supplies by 2017 – which provides jobs for the local economy, creates shorter supply chains to reduce CO_2 impacts, and improves product availability for customers.

Since 1991 Lexmark has provided customers with easy methods to return their used laser supplies through its Lexmark Cartridge Collection Program (LCCP). Free collection services cover 90 percent of customers, and presently around 30 percent are recovered, either through bins provided in offices, or prepaid postage labels. Lexmark follows a zero landfill and incineration policy for the material returned and has a goal to directly reuse

---

50 percent of the material, by weight, by 2018, with the remainder going for recycling. Used toner cartridges that are returned by customers throughout Europe are consolidated, sorted and shipped to a manufacturing facility in Poland. Using an adapted version of the new cartridge production line, cartridges with up to 90 percent of reused components can be produced. These cartridges are subject to the same quality tests, utilise the same high performance toner, and are provided with the same limited lifetime guarantee as cartridges with all new components.

The program demonstrates Lexmark's sustainability commitment, progress towards stringent long-term goals, and the ability to save material costs. Use of the recovered materials (primarily ABS polymer, which is derived from oil) means less resource extraction, less additional processing and lower supply chain impacts.

Chapter recap

Some approaches to indicators:

- **Material flow analyses (MFA)** – measures flows of materials but doesn't capture recovery.

- **Life cycle analyses (LCA)** – measures a range of impacts but expensive to do on every product.

- **Product Environmental Footprints (PEF)** – a broad-brush version of LCA useful for getting a sense of priorities, but can be criticised for not being sufficiently thorough.

- **Circular 'ability' indicators** – states whether or not a product or material can be recycled.

- **Circular use indicators** – tries to capture how far a product or material actually has been recycled.

- **Entropic overhead** – seeks to understand how best to preserve energy in the system.

- **Developments in Europe** – Europe, using business advice, is developing an agreed set of indicators.

- **What might work best?** – The easiest option is likely to be Environmentally-weighted Material Consumption (EMC), a combination of material flow analysis with environmental lifecycle analysis. A broad-brush version is hotspot analysis.

STEP 5

Making Best Use of the Brokering Organisations

IN THE UK, the closest to a circular economy 'one-stop-shop' is WRAP, the Waste and Resources Action Programme. Here is a list of other key UK-based organisations.

WRAP (www.wrap.org.uk/) provides:

- Support on food waste reduction.

- Market situation reports for key materials.

- Voluntary Responsibility initiatives such as the Courtauld Commitment.

- Research fora, such as the Product Sustainability Forum.

- Loans to support waste prevention initiatives.

The Great Recovery (www.greatrecovery.org.uk/):

- Explanation of the principles of designing for the circular economy.

- 'Tear down' events to demonstrate how everyday items can be better designed for recovery.

- Networking events.

Ellen MacArthur Foundation (www.ellenmacarthurfoundation.org/):

- Cutting-edge materials for inspiration and education.

- Conferences and seminars.

- Networking for like-minded Chief Executives and leaders.

Green Alliance (www.green-alliance.org.uk/resourcestewardship.php):

- Guidance on the principles of the circular economy.

- The Circular Economy Task Force: a business consortium advocating circular economy to government.

- Circular economy policy analysis and advocacy.

Aldersgate Group (www.aldersgategroup.org.uk/):

- An alliance of leaders from business, politics and society driving action for a sustainable economy.

- Research, analysis and networking.

- Route for collective advocacy from a large number of leading companies.

Centre for Remanufacturing and Reuse (www.remanufacturing.org.uk/ index.lasso?-session=RemanSession:569704BA0ef1e02CB3SRt2861 CD9):

- Guidance on principles of remanufacturing and reuse.

- Development of standards and certification.

- One to one support for businesses and bespoke research.

Centre for Sustainable Design (http://cfsd.org.uk/):

- Consultancy services and research for private and public sector clients.

- Training programmes.

- Events and networks.

The Resource Association (www.resourceassociation.com/home):

- Trade association for resources industry, including those collecting materials and those reprocessing them.

- Advocacy on behalf those in resources industries.

- Collaborative working with like-minded bodies.

The Environment Agency (https://www.gov.uk/browse/environment-countryside/recycling-waste-management):

- Guidance on meeting all waste regulations, including whether something should be treated as a 'waste' or not, or can be considered a 'product'.

- Guidance and regulation of producer responsibility laws.

- Guidance on industrial process efficiency.

Chartered Institute of Waste Managers (CIWM – www.ciwm.co.uk/CIWM/CIWMHome.aspx):

- A professional institute for those involved in resources issues – open to chartered waste managers and others.

- Route for policy input and advocacy.

- Provides professional development, networking.

Environmental Services Association (Trade Association for the Waste and Resources Industries – **www.esauk.org/**):

- Information and statistics about the waste and resources industries.

- Route for collective policy input and advocacy.

- Support, events and networking for members.

Engineering Employers Federation (EEF – **www.eef.org.uk/**):

- Guidance on implications and benefit of circular economy for manufacturers.

- Survey material.

- Events and networking for members.

Conclusion

CIRCULAR ECONOMY sounds daunting, but once it is understood that it is complete system involving all actors in the supply chain, you are on the way to understanding your company's part in that system. You can then define where you can affect change, and where you will need help to create change. The starting point can be raising awareness in supply chains, followed by a simple hotspot analysis that shows three or four key areas of impact. The next stage is tackling product design internally, or externally with suppliers – how the product might be reconfigured to tackle those problem areas. If your product can't easily be re-used, remanufactured or recycled you can set a timetable for when that might be possible.

Key to getting the initiative off the ground is buy-in from all the main players, preferably all the way up to the board. Reasons to act include defending the company from resource risks, capturing more value from the products and materials that pass through your hands, and securing environmental benefits. And if you feel that the company has reached the limits of what it can achieve, and reaping further benefits involves broader stimuli such as standards, legislation or government financial support – say so, loud and clear. Most of all, this is a complex and evolving area of debate, so don't expect it to stand still!

Action check list

Have you:

- Briefed yourself on the key terms and concepts of the circular economy? (See Step 1.)

- Briefed yourself on the benefits seen by other companies? (See Step 2.)

  - saving money

  - opening up new areas of business

  - prompting innovation

  - avoiding risks

  - improving the firm's reputation

- If these case studies don't seem sufficiently applicable to your business, have you sought out other examples?

- Thought about what your business does and how it does it? (See Step 3.)

- Thought about where there might be opportunities to:

  - change your business model so that the priority is the delivery of value and service, rather than the quantity of product sold?

  - use resources more efficiently in the course of delivering your service or product?

  - recover more of the resources you use, or enable others to do so?

- design for better recovery in the future?

- partner with others to achieve these goals, if they are difficult to achieve on your own?

- Having identified opportunities, have you:

  - set them out in a way that will be compelling to colleagues?

  - identified who in your organisation could help take them forward, and set up appropriate briefings?

  - anticipated the barriers that might be presented, and assembled the arguments to answer them? (See Step 3.)

  - used the techniques and the free assessment tools mentioned in Step 4 to confirm your initial thoughts and help you move forwards?

  - made full use of the brokering organisations mentioned in Step 5 to support you in building a case and working out the practicalities?

  - come back to the arguments, and made them in different ways, if you don't get a favourable reception at first?

  - made sure the door is at least open for you to provide colleagues with updates and further briefing?

  - sought out like-minded colleagues in other organisations who can give you support while you are trying to effect change in your own organisation?

References

The Performance Economy (www.palgrave.com/page/detail/the-performance-economy-walter-r-stahel/?K=9780230584662)

Resource Resilient UK (www.green-alliance.org.uk/uploadedFiles/Publications/reports/Resource%20resilient%20UK_a%20report%20from%20the%20circular%20economy%20task%20force%20.pdf)

Cradle to Cradle (www.amazon.co.uk/Cradle-Michael-Braungart/dp/0099535475)

The Secret Life of Stuff (www.amazon.co.uk/The-Secret-Life-Stuff-Material/dp/0099546582)

Towards the Circular Economy (www.ellenmacarthurfoundation.org/business/reports)

Reinventing the Wheel (www.green-alliance.org.uk/page_77.php)

The Great Recovery (www.greatrecovery.org.uk/the-great-recovery-report/)